THE CIVIL WAR

Scott Marquette

Rourke Publishing LLC
Vero Beach, Florida 32964

Rourke
Publishing LLC

PHOTO CREDITS:
Army Center of Military History: cover, pages 8, 14, 18, 20, 33; Defense Visual Information Center: pages 6, 10, 12, 16, 22, 26, 28, 29, 30, 32, 34, 36, 40, 42; Library of Congress, pages 21, 38; AP/Wide World Photo: 4, 24, 44.

PRODUCED by Lownik Communication Services, Inc. www.lcs-impact.com
DESIGNED by Cunningham Design

Library of Congress Cataloging-in-Publication Data

Marquette, Scott.
  The Civil War / Scott Marquette.
      p. cm. – (America at war)
Summary: Discusses the events of the conflict between northern and southern states in the mid-nineteenth century, a war in which more than one million men died or were wounded.
  Includes bibliographical references (p. 45) and index.
  ISBN 1-58952-388-1
  1. United States–History–Civil War, 1861-1865–Juvenile literature.
[1. United States–History–Civil War, 1861-1865.] I. Title. II. America at war (Rourke Publishing)
  E468 .M22 2002
  973.7–dc21

                            2002001240

Printed in the USA

Cover Image:
Union troops attack the Confederate lines at
Vicksburg, Mississippi, on May 19, 1863.

Table of Contents

In the Civil War, Americans fought each other over the issues of slavery and states' rights.

Americans Fighting Americans

From 1861 to 1865, America fought a bloody war. But the war was not against a foreign nation. Instead, Americans killed each other. More than a million men died or were hurt in the Civil War. The nation was torn apart. The president was killed by an assassin. Many people think the war was the most important event in our history.

Why did they fight? How did the United States almost split in two? Why did friends—and even family—go to war with each other? The reasons go to the heart of American ideals. Men on both sides fought for freedom and justice. But they had very different ideas about what those words meant.

The war brought to an end a terrible crime: human slavery in the United States of America. But ending that crime cost thousands of lives. The Civil War left scars that still last today.

The North fought the war to preserve the Union and keep the country together. It also fought to end slavery.

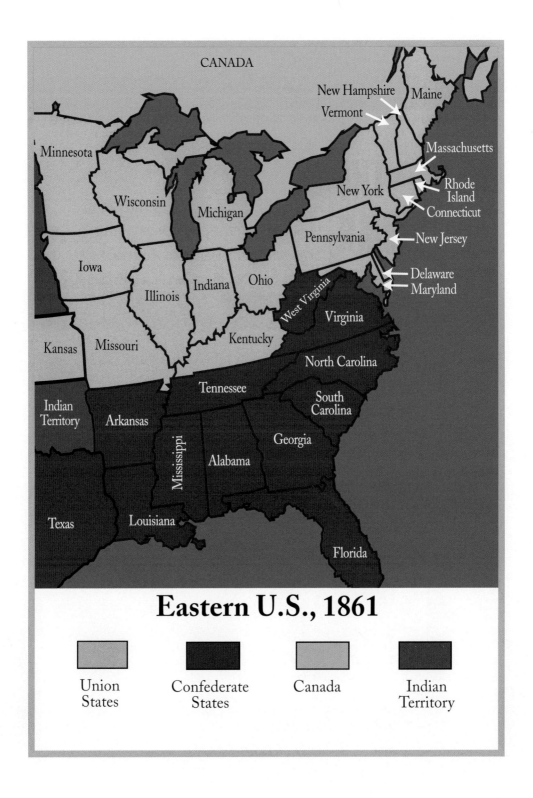

Eastern U.S., 1861

Union States | Confederate States | Canada | Indian Territory

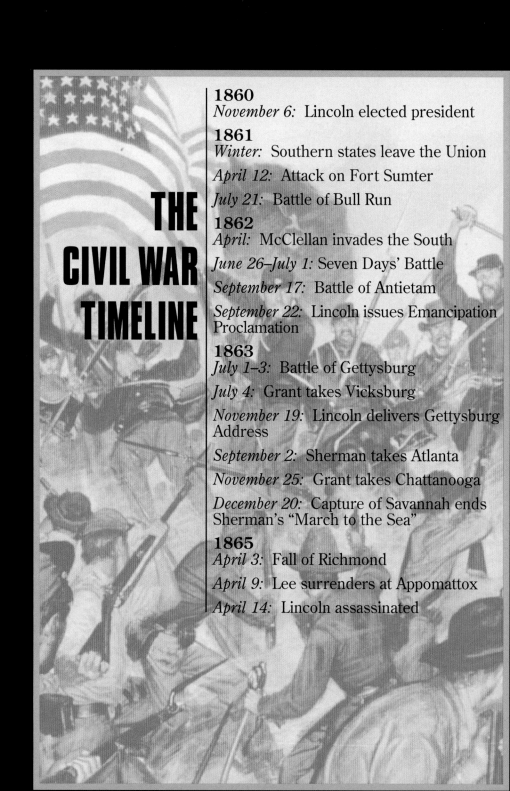

THE CIVIL WAR TIMELINE

1860

November 6: Lincoln elected president

1861

Winter: Southern states leave the Union

April 12: Attack on Fort Sumter

July 21: Battle of Bull Run

1862

April: McClellan invades the South

June 26–July 1: Seven Days' Battle

September 17: Battle of Antietam

September 22: Lincoln issues Emancipation Proclamation

1863

July 1–3: Battle of Gettysburg

July 4: Grant takes Vicksburg

November 19: Lincoln delivers Gettysburg Address

September 2: Sherman takes Atlanta

November 25: Grant takes Chattanooga

December 20: Capture of Savannah ends Sherman's "March to the Sea"

1865

April 3: Fall of Richmond

April 9: Lee surrenders at Appomattox

April 14: Lincoln assassinated

A Nation Divided

In the years before the Civil War, life was different in the northern United States than in the southern. In the South, life was based on farming. Very large farms, called **plantations**, grew crops to sell for cash. Cotton was the chief crop. It was so important to the South, people called it "King Cotton." The South did not have many factories.

It took many people to do the hard work of raising cotton. To have enough labor, most plantations used **slaves**. Africans had been brought to America as slaves since the 1600s. They were bought and sold like animals. A master could beat, or even kill, a slave. It was a crime to teach slaves to read or write. A few slaves were freed by their masters. Some escaped. A few more bought their own freedom. But most remained slaves their whole lives. By 1860 there were more than four million slaves in America.

Most people in the North also lived on farms. But there were few large plantations. More and more people lived in cities. Some worked in factories. Many people in the North were opposed to slavery. They believed it was wrong for one

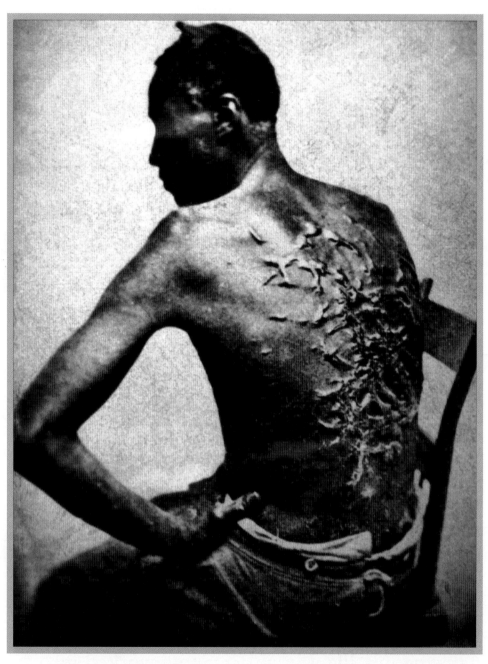

Before the Civil War, more than four million African Americans were kept as slaves. This man had been whipped cruelly by his master.

person to own another. People who tried to end slavery were called **abolitionists**. Slavery was against the law in many states in the North.

The debate over slavery heated up in the 1840s and 1850s. More people were settling in the West. New states were being formed. Congress argued about allowing slavery in the new states. The North wanted the new areas to stay free. The South wanted states to decide about slavery for themselves.

More people started to side with the abolitionists. A new political party, the Republican Party, was formed to end slavery. In 1860, it chose Abraham Lincoln to run for president. Leaders in the South warned they would not put up with Lincoln as president. But Lincoln won the election by a slim margin.

Abraham Lincoln

As a boy, Abraham Lincoln lived in a log cabin. He loved to read and grew up to be a lawyer. People admired Lincoln for his intelligence and honesty. Today, he is remembered as the man who freed the slaves and held the nation together.

Abraham Lincoln ran for president opposing slavery. His election angered many in the South.

Days later, South Carolina **seceded**. It declared that it was no longer part of the United States. Other states in the South did the same. In February 1861, these states formed the **Confederate States of America**. There were a few desperate attempts to avoid war. Leaders from the North and South met to find a way out. But on April 12, 1861, Confederates fired cannon at Fort Sumter in South Carolina. The Civil War had begun.

The huge loss of life in the first battles of the Civil War showed it would go on for a long time.

Delays and Defeats

When war broke out, people on both sides thought it would be short. People in the North believed they would quickly beat the South. Southerners thought the North would soon tire of war and leave the **Confederacy** alone.

They soon learned how wrong they were. The first major battle of the war was fought on July 21, 1861. The two armies met at Bull Run, Virginia. People came from Washington to watch a great victory. But the **Union** troops were poorly trained. The Confederates beat them. But the southern army was too weak to pursue its retreating foe.

After Bull Run, both sides knew it would be a long war. North and South raised large armies. Lincoln put General George McClellan in charge of the Union army. McClellan was popular with the men. But he insisted he needed more time and more troops. Lincoln urged him to attack.

At last, in spring 1862, McClellan moved his men into Virginia. His plan was to take the Confederate capital of Richmond. But he was met by many delays. He faced strong resistance on the way. Before he could attack Richmond, troops had to be sent to meet a new threat.

General McClellan's army defeated the South at Antietam Creek, shown in this photo. It was one of the first real victories for the North.

The South tried to capture the capital of its enemy, too. General Stonewall Jackson led a lightning raid on Union troops at Harpers Ferry, Virginia. It looked like the South might take Washington. But Jackson moved his army to Richmond instead. There, Southern **cavalry** attacked the Union army. Under General Robert E. Lee, the South drove McClellan's troops back. The fight, called the Seven Days' Battle, was one more big loss for the Union.

A second battle at Bull Run in August saw another Union defeat. Lee then crossed the Potomac River. The fight was now on northern soil. At last, the North got a break. McClellan secretly got Lee's battle plans. He met Lee's army at **Antietam** Creek. The Union won a narrow victory. But McClellan let Lee's army get away.

Towns Wiped Out

At times, army units were formed by the soldiers from the same town. In the battles, tens of thousands of soldiers could be killed in one day. This meant that sometimes almost all men from a town were killed in one terrible battle.

In the second Battle of Bull Run, the North suffered a bitter defeat.

The Battle of Antietam was the first bright spot for the North. Lincoln took the chance to issue a historic order. He declared that all slaves in the South were free. The **Emancipation Proclamation** would end slavery in the United States. But first, the Union would have to win the war.

At the Battle of Gettysburg, Lee tried over and over to break the Union line. He failed and the South's last major invasion of the North was defeated.

The Tide Turns

Lee's army had fought well. But the South was desperate. It was running out of men and supplies. Lee needed a major victory, one that might end the war. He hoped the North would tire and quit.

In the spring of 1863, Lee crossed the Potomac again. The North feared he might take Washington. The Union army went to stop him. The two sides met in Gettysburg, Pennsylvania, on July 1. For three days, Lee tried to break the Union line. Each time he was pushed back. In the end, after heavy losses, Lee was forced to retreat. The Battle of Gettysburg was one of the bloodiest of the war. More than 50,000 soldiers lost their lives.

The next day, the North had another big victory. The Union general, Ulysses S. Grant, tried to get control of the Mississippi River.

Abraham Lincoln's handwritten copy of his Gettysburg Address

This photo of the battlefield at Gettysburg was taken shortly after the battle. Lincoln's speech at this battlefield was one of the most important in American history.

Grant put the town of Vicksburg, Mississippi, under **siege**. For three months, the army shelled the town. Troops stopped any food or supplies from entering. At last, on July 4, Vicksburg fell. The victory split the Confederacy.

That fall, Grant's troops pushed into Tennessee. Though the southern army was smaller, it fought back hard. But Grant was not to be stopped. It took two months, but he finally captured Chattanooga in November. It was an important **rail hub** for the South. The Confederates now had an even harder time getting supplies.

In November, Lincoln spoke at the battlefield in Gettysburg. His speech was short. He said the war would give the country "a new birth of freedom." The Union was fighting for equality, just like the nation's founders. The Union must win to save democracy, he said.

Robert E. Lee

General Lee was the South's greatest soldier. He did not want the South to leave the Union. But he decided he had to serve his home state of Virginia. His leadership kept the southern cause alive.

General Robert E. Lee led the Confederate army through a series of military victories. But he eventually lost the war.

The Gettysburg Address was one of Lincoln's greatest speeches.

The Confederacy was starting to fail. In 1864, Grant cut through Virginia. His plan now was to wage a war of **attrition**. He destroyed crops, supplies, and rail lines. The South was also losing many soldiers. Grant wanted to make the South unable to fight. At last, the Union laid siege to the Confederate capital of Richmond. For the South, the end was at hand.

The Union blockade kept the South from buying goods like ammunition, shoes, and salt.

Daily Life during the War

Most Americans, in both the North and the South, lived on farms. For most, the war was remote. Except for soldiers, few people actually saw fighting. But almost every person was touched by the Civil War.

Life was hardest in the South. Because the Confederacy had few factories, it had to buy many goods. It used crops like cotton to raise cash. But the Union navy set up a **blockade**. It stopped ships from entering or leaving. The South could not sell its cotton. Without cash, many people became desperately poor. Food, cloth, and other goods were scarce. What little

The Bloodiest War

The Civil War was the nation's most deadly war. New kinds of rifles and cannon had increased accuracy. This made the old ways of war, like charging an enemy, very deadly. As a result, more men died in the Civil War than in all the nation's other wars combined.

Iron-clad gunboats like this one prevented southern states from selling their cotton to other countries.

there was had to be used to support the war effort.

In 1864, the Union war of attrition brought more misery. Farms and cities in the South were burned. Railroads and bridges were destroyed. Many **civilians** died. Cities like Richmond and Atlanta were heavily damaged. Nearly all the men—even boys—went to fight. Tens of thousands never returned.

For people in the North, life was easier. Most of the fighting was in the South. The North did not

Both South and North relied on trains for transportation. Both armies destroyed train tracks to cripple the enemy.

see such poverty. More factories were built. Cities grew. But the loss of men was keenly felt. Farms went untended. Public support for the war was high at first. But later, Union losses caused many people to question the war. A **draft** was imposed to force men to join the army.

Some people in the North tried to stop the war. Some did not believe that slaves should be freed. Others thought saving the Union was not worth so many deaths. These **copperheads** protested the

The destruction of the Civil War forced many people to flee their homes.

draft. They even helped southern prisoners to escape. Copperheads ran a candidate to oppose Lincoln. He was George McClellan—the general who had once been head of the army! The copperheads caused great division in the North. Riots broke out in some cities.

The war did more damage in the South than in the North. But on both sides, people sacrificed. They gave up freedoms and lost loved ones. The scars of the war changed America forever.

*Sherman's march through Georgia
left the state in ruins.*

"The Grapes of Wrath"

As the Confederacy weakened, the North continued its war of attrition. Grant's idea was to ruin the will of the South to fight. He wanted to leave the southern army without food or supplies. He hoped this would end the war quickly.

Grant sent an army under General William Sherman to destroy the South. He marched to Atlanta, Georgia, the heart of the Confederacy. His army burned, stole, or wrecked everything in its path. On September 2, 1864, Sherman captured Atlanta. He forced the civilians there to leave. Then his men set the city on fire. After a rest, the army marched to the sea. It left behind a trail of

Northern troops moved relentlessly through the South in the final months of the war.

*General William Tecumseh Sherman led his troops
on a mission to destroy southern towns. Thousands of slaves
abandoned their masters and followed the Union soldiers.*

destruction 60 miles (96 kilometers) wide. Anything the army could not use it destroyed. On December 20, Sherman captured the city of Savannah. He offered it to Lincoln as a Christmas present. The North had taken one of the South's last seaports. The heart of the Confederacy lay in ruins.

Meanwhile, Grant kept up his siege of Richmond. The city's population began to starve. Through the winter, Lee's army defended the city. But in the spring, fighting in the West caused Lee to leave the city. The civilians were forced to flee. Grant's troops took Richmond on April 3, 1865, as fires raged through the town.

Now Lee's army was trapped. Grant's troops were north of him. Sherman was to the south. Lee's once mighty army had dwindled to a few thousand

Deadly Inventions

New inventions played an important part in the Civil War. Rifled muskets and cannon had spiral grooves inside to make them more accurate. The first warships with armor plates were used. Torpedoes were used to sink ships.

*General Lee surrendered to General Grant at Appomattox
Courthouse on April 9, 1865.*

men. Lee tried to fight on. Grant chased the remains of the Confederate Army through Virginia. Finally, Lee knew he was beaten. He sent word to Grant that he would surrender.

On April 9, the two men met at Appomattox Courthouse to discuss the terms of surrender. Grant was very generous. He knew that, after all the killing, he must start to heal the wounds of war. He could have taken Lee's soldiers prisoner. Instead, if Lee's men gave up their arms and agreed not to fight, Grant would let them go home. He even let the men keep their horses. Lee agreed to Grant's terms. The Civil War was over.

SURRAT. BOOTH. HAROLD.

War Department, Washington, April 20, 1865,

 $100,000 REWARD!

THE MURDERER

Of our late beloved President, Abraham Lincoln,

IS STILL AT LARGE.

$50,000 REWARD

Will be paid by this Department for his apprehension, in addition to any reward offered by Municipal Authorities or State Executives.

$25,000 REWARD

Will be paid for the apprehension of JOHN H. SURRATT, one of Booth's Accomplices.

$25,000 REWARD

Will be paid for the apprehension of David C. Harold, another of Booth's accomplices.

LIBERAL REWARDS will be paid for any information that shall conduce to the arrest of either of the above-named criminals, or their accomplices.

All persons harboring or secreting the said persons, or either of them, or aiding or assisting their concealment or escape, will be treated as accomplices in the murder of the President and the attempted assassination of the Secretary of

President Lincoln was shot and killed by John Wilkes Booth, an actor who was angry that the South had lost the Civil War.

The Nation Slowly Heals

At the war's end, many people in the North wanted revenge. They wanted to punish the South for the war. But Lincoln did not agree. He knew that the nation must now come together. Lincoln wanted to be easy on the South and bind the nation's wounds.

Sadly, he never got the chance. On April 14, 1865, Lincoln was shot. His murderer, John Wilkes Booth, was an actor. He was angry that the Union had won the war. He killed Lincoln as the president was watching a play. The nation was shocked. It was the first time a president was **assassinated**.

With Lincoln dead, Congress was in the hands of those who hated the South. It passed the 14th Amendment to the Constitution. This made former slaves U.S. citizens. But Congress also passed the **Reconstruction Act**. It did not accept the southern states back in the Union. Instead, the act set up military occupation. Former Confederate leaders were barred from serving in government.

Ulysses S. Grant was a popular figure after the war.
He eventually became president of the United States.

Slowly, the South began to rebuild. The slaves were free. But they were still very poor. Most had no education. Plantations, which needed slave labor, vanished. Instead, landowners rented land to poor farmers and got a large share of their crops in return. The early years of freedom brought more poverty and hard work to the former slaves. They did not have the same rights as white people. It was the start of a long, slow journey to full equality.

As time went on, the former Confederate states were taken back into the Union. The South rebuilt its cities and farms. More African Americans moved north. The South built more factories. Life became less different in the North and South. But the South resented the war and Reconstruction for a long time.

Today, we still live in the shadow of the Civil War. African Americans still struggle for fairness

Ulysses S. Grant

When the Civil War started, Ulysses S. Grant joined the Army as a clerk. But his sharp mind was noticed. He became an officer and then a general. Four years after the war, he was elected president.

*After the Civil War, the South faced the huge task of
rebuilding its ruined cities.*

and opportunity. We still argue about how power-
ful the states should be. But we are more united
as a people. We share common values, and a
common way of life. Never again have Americans
waged war on each other.

The Civil War was the deadliest war in U.S. history.
The scars from the war still last today.

Further Reading

Hakim, Joy. *War, Terrible War*. Oxford University Press, 1999.

Herbert, Janis. *The Civil War for Kids*. Chicago Review Press, 1999.

Moore, Kay. *If You Lived at the Time of the Civil War*. Scholastic, 1994.

Murphy, Jim. *The Boys' War: Confederate and Union Soldiers Talk About the Civil War*. Clarion Books, 1993.

Rappaport, Doreen. *Escape from Slavery: Five Journeys to Freedom*. Harper Trophy, 1999.

Websites to Visit
AmericanCivilWar.com
www.americancivilwar.com

Home of the American Civil War
www.civilwarhome.com

Library of Congress Civil War Photography Collection
www.lcweb.loc.gov/spcoll/048.html

Glossary

abolitionists — people who worked to end slavery

Antietam — a village in Maryland that was the scene of one of the bloodiest battles in the Civil War

assassinated — murdered, often for political reasons

attrition — weakening an enemy

blockade — use of ships to keep goods from entering or leaving a country

cavalry — soldiers mounted on horses

civilians — people not enlisted in the military

Confederacy — name for the southern states in the Civil War

Confederate States of America — the union of southern states that seceded from the United States

copperheads — northerners opposed to the war, so called for the pennies they wore as a badge

draft — a law that forces people to serve in the military

Emancipation Proclamation — Lincoln's order to free (or emancipate) the slaves

plantations — large farms that grow crops to sell for cash

rail hub — a central point for railroad transportation

Reconstruction Act — the northern plan to punish the South after the war

rifled — a gun barrel with a circular groove cut inside; the groove made the shell spin, giving the gun greater accuracy

seceded — withdrew from union with the United States

siege — the surrounding of a city or fort by an army

slaves — humans bought and sold as workers

Union — name for the northern side in the Civil War; the bond between American states

Index